A Wrongful Death in Ohio

Actions Families Can Take After the Wrongful Death of a Loved One

Slater & Zurz LLP, Attorneys at Law
Serving Clients Throughout Ohio
Office Locations:
Akron • Canton • Cleveland • Columbus

A Wrongful Death in Ohio
By: Slater & Zurz LLP
Attorneys at Law

©Copyright 2018 by Slater & Zurz LLP

All rights reserved. This book or any portion thereof may not be reproduced or used in any manner whatsoever without the express written permission of Slater & Zurz LLP.

Printed in the United States of America

First Printing 2014

For permission to reproduce or to order additional copies of this book, contact Slater & Zurz LLP by calling 1-800-297-9191 or visit our websites:

slaterzurz.com
ohiowrongfuldeathlaw.com

Table of Contents

Foreword   1

Introduction   3

Chapter 1   8
Understanding Wrongful Death

Chapter 2   12
The Potential Losses and Damages Recoverable in a Wrongful Death Claim

Chapter 3   18
When a Wrongful Death Claim is Caused by Two or More Parties

Chapter 4   20
Wrongful Death of a Child

Chapter 5   23
Wrongful Death from an Auto Accident

Chapter 6 25

Wrongful Death from a Defective Product

Chapter 7 27

Wrongful Death from Explosions

Chapter 8 29

Determining the Value of a Wrongful Death Case

Chapter 9 36

Loss of Consortium and How it Factors into Wrongful Death Cases

Chapter 10 39

Filing a Wrongful Death Claim with an Insurance Company

Chapter 11 54

How Wrongful Death Cases are Litigated

Chapter 12 68

Contingency Fee Agreements with Attorneys

The Authors 71

Foreword

By Jim Slater, Managing Partner, Slater & Zurz LLP

I bring to this subject more than 40 years of experience representing families when they lost their child, wife, husband, grandfather or grandmother because someone did something wrong. In each case, the greatest upset and heartbreak I have had to endure with a family is grappling with the fact that it did not have to happen.

These are difficult times indeed, but by taking legal action with an experienced law firm you may be able to prevent such a tragedy from happening again to another family. Whether it is a trucking company, a driver of an automobile, a doctor or a nursing home, we are extremely aggressive in our efforts to seek the largest financial punishment possible.

While money cannot bring back the child, wife, husband or grandparent, it can make where and how we live safer, because payments of large sums by people and or companies that do bad things can elicit behavior changes for the better and those changes have the power to make our society safer.

I understand it is tough for you right now. Please email me directly at jslater@slaterzurz.com, call me at my office (1-800-297-9191) or reach out to me on my cell phone (330-

701-6111). People find that a brief conversation with me can be very helpful. Let God be with you and bring peace to your life.

Introduction

The sudden or unexpected death of a loved one is a tragic experience. When the loved one's death is a result of the carelessness or negligence of another individual, a business or an organization, it is inexcusable.

Death in and of itself creates strong emotions of loss and sadness. It may also produce feelings of bewilderment and extreme anxiety regarding your family's future. No one could ever be prepared for such an overwhelming event.

If you are reading this book because you lost a loved one as the result of an auto accident, medical error or some other type of unfortunate event, we offer our sincere sympathies. During the past 40-plus years of practicing law, we have seen how a wrongful death can impact a family and it is why we fight so hard for clients in these cases.

This book is intended to help you understand wrongful death and provide general guidance on actions your family can take to hold the party (or parties) accountable for their actions, including your right to recover fair monetary compensation for your loss.

Of course, no amount of money could ever make up for the loss of a loved one. It is important, however, that a family prepare for how it will change their lives and their futures. There will be emotional changes and financial uncertainties. Ohio law recognizes this fact and allows for the recovery of monetary compensation for a wrongful death.

Filing and pursuing a claim can be an extremely complicated and cumbersome process. It requires a thorough understanding of many types of Ohio laws. In addition, the expense associated with a wrongful death case can be significant.

These types of cases usually require in-depth investigations as well as testimony from various types of experts. To prevail in a wrongful death case, it typically is necessary to hire a range of professionals to help prove the various aspects of your case.

For these reasons and more, it is advisable to speak with an Ohio-licensed attorney who has significant experience handling wrongful death cases. It should also be an attorney who possesses all the necessary resources and skills to pursue a case all the way to a trial. And it should be an attorney who knows when it is in the client's best interest to settle a case prior to going to a trial.

Wrongful death claims are considered high-priority claims for insurance companies. Indeed, they usually assign their most experienced and effective insurance adjusters to them. This is a tactic insurance companies use to fight against a claim or to minimize the court-ordered payout.

Dealing with a veteran insurance adjuster without the guidance or assistance of an experienced Ohio attorney can find you in a situation that does not serve your best interests.

We endeavored to write this book to give families a thorough understanding of what a wrongful death claim is all about, and the knowledge they need to determine if they should consider pursuing one.

While no amount of money in the world will ever replace your loved one, it has been our experience that clients gain a sense of closure after acting in a wrongful death case. It enables them to move on and continue to live life with a sense that some amount of justice, and therefore peace, has been found.

If you are considering pursuing such a claim, we invite you to contact us for a free, no-obligation consultation and case evaluation.

Our free consultations are relaxed conversations in which we review the details of your case, answer your questions and provide you with the benefit of our guidance based on many decades of experience.

The free consultation can take place over the telephone or in a face-to-face meeting if you prefer. Upon completion of the free consultation, you will be under no obligation to hire our law firm. We simply look forward to hearing from you.

Slater & Zurz LLP
Akron • Canton • Cleveland • Columbus

Call for a free consultation with our experienced attorneys: 1-800-297-9191
slaterzurz.com
ohiowrongfuldeathlaw.com

DISCLAIMER

The information contained within this book is for informational use only.

This book is not intended to be used as legal advice. No attorney-client relationship has been developed or created because of receiving, purchasing or reading this book.

Cases involving wrongful death can be complex and involve many different legal issues, where the outcome of any litigation is dependent on the particulars of that unique and specific case.

You should consult with a qualified Ohio attorney who is both licensed and experienced with wrongful death cases in the state of Ohio.

If you would like a free consultation with an attorney at the Ohio law firm of Slater & Zurz LLP, please call us at 1-800-297-9191 or visit slaterzurz.com and send a message from our website.

Chapter 1
Understanding a Wrongful Death

A death that is "wrongful" is one that is caused by the negligence or unlawful act of another person, persons, business or organization. The erroneous conduct can, under the law, be either intentional or unintentional.

A wrongful death case refers to the type of personal injury claim that may be brought on behalf of certain surviving relatives to recover compensation against the party or parties responsible for causing the death of a family member.

A single person or multiple individuals can cause a wrongful death. It can also be caused by a non-person, such as a local business, corporation or governmental entity. Additionally, the cause of a death can be the combination of a person and a nonperson. For example, an employee and his or her company may be identified as the responsible parties in these types of legal claims.

When a wrongful death occurs, an action against the responsible party or parties may be pursued in the name of the estate of the deceased.

Most wrongful death claims are based on the act of negligence committed by the responsible party or parties. The term "negligence" is defined as "the failure to exercise ordinary care under the same or similar circumstances." Therefore, to prove a claim, you must show that the person or persons who caused the death were acting carelessly in some way.

Sometimes, it can be easy to conclude whether a person was negligent, and that the negligence resulted in another person's death. In other circumstances, it can be very challenging to determine.

Civil Responsibility vs. Criminal Responsibility

There is a distinct and important difference between civil and criminal liability in wrongful death cases. A civil claim will involve only the recovery of money against the responsible party or parties.

Often the party accused of causing the death is defended by an insurance company. In a civil claim, the primary challenge is in determining what amount of money must be paid to compensate the surviving relatives. The party or parties responsible will only be required to pay money, not be sentenced to serve jail time in a civil case.

A person who is found to have caused a wrongful death may also be criminally responsible. The responsible party or parties must have acted intentionally or recklessly to be guilty of a crime. If criminal liability does exist, the responsible party or parties may in fact be sentenced to prison.

Although a claim may be brought against a person who kills another, the claim may not be worth pursuing because there is no insurance policy to pay a settlement or verdict. Discussing the details of the case with an Ohio attorney experienced with wrongful death cases will help in determining if a claim can and should be pursued.

Time Limits to File a Wrongful Death Claim

There exist strictly defined time limits on when a wrongful death case may be filed or pursued. This is referred to as the Statute of Limitations.

In Ohio, the Statute of Limitations is typically two (2) years from the date of death. This means that the case must either be settled or filed in court within this time frame or the claim is no longer valid.

It is not advisable to wait until the end of the two-year period before filing a suit or a claim but rather to begin investigating a case immediately following the person's death.

An insurance company or companies will likely contest your claim. You need to take necessary actions to support and prove your wrongful death claim. This may include gathering witness statements, performing an accident reconstruction, obtaining a private autopsy, and hiring the appropriate experts. Prompt investigations can dramatically increase the likelihood of a case being successful.

Chapter 2
The Potential Losses and Damages Recoverable in a Wrongful Death Claim

Perhaps the last thing on your mind when a family member dies is how much you and your family can be compensated for a loved one's death. In fact, assigning an amount of money to your family member's life may seem either impossible or distasteful.

The fact remains, however, that you and your family suffered a loss as a result of your loved one's death and it is imperative to prepare and plan for your future. Oftentimes the only justice that can be achieved under the law for such a tragic loss is an award of monetary compensation.

While the financial award granted in a wrongful death claim will not ease the pain of loss, it can help families move forward in their grieving process and in other aspects of their lives. It can also provide a sense of closure and help you put the past behind you and move on.

A wrongful death claim can be brought in Ohio within two (2) years of the date of death. The aim of Ohio law is to achieve compensation for the survivors, as if the decedent had not died and continued to be there for them providing support and companionship. Compensatory damages are permitted in Ohio, and they can be awarded in the following instances:

(1) Loss of support from the reasonably expected earning capacity of the decedent;

(2) Loss of services of the decedent;

(3) Loss of the society of the decedent, including loss of companionship, consortium, care, assistance, attention, protection, advice, guidance, counsel, instruction, training, and education, suffered by the surviving spouse, dependent children, parents, or next-of-kin of the decedent;

(4) Loss of prospective inheritance to the decedent's heirs at the time of the decedent's death;

(5) The mental anguish incurred by the surviving spouse, dependent children, parents or next of kin of the decedent.

Ohio law states that only certain types of damages may be recoverable in a wrongful death case. Generally, the damages are divided into two categories—economic and non-economic. The damages in both categories can be recovered by the estate of the deceased in Ohio.

Economic damages refer to amounts that are easier to calculate. This includes items such as lost earnings, medical expenses, and other forms of what are referred to as compensatory damages.

Non-economic damages refer to more intangible losses. These are defined as subjective losses and include pain, suffering, grief, mental anguish, and the loss of the relationship with the deceased.

Damages Recoverable by the Estate of the Deceased

Again, the deceased's estate may recover both economic and non-economic damages.

The following is a list of common types of damages for the estate:

> **(1) Health care and funeral expenses.** The cost of medical treatment the deceased received prior to their death can be very high when the person required hospital emergency room care and/or emergency surgery to save his or her life.

These claim amounts are typically offset by the amounts paid by Medicare, Medicaid, or private health insurance companies.

Funeral expenses are also recoverable under the law. This can include mortuary services, a casket, transportation to the burial site, costs of cremation, the purchase of a grave site, the expense of a headstone, and other similar expenses.

> **(2) Loss of net earnings.** The future net earnings the deceased was projected to earn over his or her working life can also be recovered. This is calculated by subtracting the amount of money the deceased would have used for personal consumption or personal expenses from the gross projected earnings over his or her lifetime. These sorts of calculations must be made by a recognized professional such as an economist and then reduced to present value.

If the deceased individual died before his or her prime career earning years, they may not have realized their full earning potential prior to their untimely death.

For example, if the deceased was a physician just beginning his or her career there may be a dispute over how much money they could have earned over the course of their career. For someone in the medical field such as a doctor, the amount could be significant.

More often, it is easier to calculate the deceased's future net earnings when the individual was an adult rather than a child. In the case of a child, there is always speculation regarding how much money he or she may have earned. Sometimes it may be necessary to rely on the financial earning history of the parents and siblings to get a sense of how financially successful the child may or may not have been, had the child survived to a normal life expectancy.

> **(3) Pain and suffering.** If the deceased person experienced pain, or suffered prior to their death, and this can be proved, the estate may claim damages for this type of non-economic loss.

In cases involving instantaneous death, the estate may not recover for pain and suffering. These types of damages are only available if measurable time elapses between injury and death. So how is it possible to know if a deceased person experienced pain before death?

To answer that question witnesses who were present or witnessed the death are utilized. If no witnesses can be produced, professional experts such as medical doctors can offer opinions on whether the deceased likely experienced pain or suffered prior to their death.

Damages Recoverable by the Beneficiaries

Certain designated surviving relatives may recover individual damages for the death of a family member. Here are some common types of damages that may be recovered by a beneficiary of a wrongful death victim:

(1) **Past and future economic benefits.** The surviving family members may recover many types of economic value they would have received from the deceased—from the date of the death through the deceased's life expectancy including money, goods and services.

For example, if the deceased had minor children at the time of their death and was expected to pay for the children's school and college education, then this expense may be recoverable.

(2) **Loss of consortium.** This term refers to the fact that each surviving family member has a claim for the loss of his or her relationship with the deceased. In the case of a surviving spouse the damages are for the loss of the deceased's company, cooperation, emotional support, love, affection, care, services, and companionship.

Wrongful death cases can be complicated legal matters because of the many different types of potential damages involved.

Chapter 3
What Happens When Wrongful Death is Caused by Two or More Parties?

Any wrongful death claim can become confusing when only one party is responsible for the death. Yet when two or more parties are involved, there are often additional problems to resolve. Sometimes it is difficult to determine who should legally share in what is termed "joint and several liability."

Professionals can investigate how the death occurred and help decide which parties are responsible. In some cases, parties do not knowingly act together, and one may not even know they caused a death.

In a case where more than one party is responsible for a death, a single individual will not be required to bear the entire liability unless he or she is responsible for the majority of the economic loss. In Ohio, non-economic losses are still assigned proportionately. This means that if the jury finds that someone is 10 percent responsible for non-economic loss, he or she is obligated to pay 10 percent of the amount the jury awarded. The share each responsible party must pay is based on varying degrees of legal responsibility.

Chapter 4
Wrongful Death of a Child

Few events in life are more tragic than the death of a child. Clearly no amount of money will ever bring back the child or make up for such a devastatingly sad loss.

Nevertheless, the law recognizes such a claim and gives a parent specific rights against the responsible party. The recovery of monetary compensation may play a part in holding the responsible party accountable for the death and prevent a similar occurrence from happening to another child in the future. A wrongful death claim may also help the parents throughout their grieving and healing process.

Ohio authorizes a parent to recover damages for the loss of a minor child if the parent has regularly contributed to the support of that child.

The issue of whether a parent regularly contributed to the support of their child is considered legally as a question of fact. This indicates that there is no specific definition of what it means to regularly contribute to the support of the child. Any determination will depend on the specific facts of the case. In the end, a judge or jury will weigh the evidence and the facts to determine whether a parent has proven that he or she supported the child during the child's lifetime.

Wrongful Death of an Unborn Fetus

Ohio wrongful death laws apply to an unborn fetus if the fetus was viable. Usually a viable fetus is one that was healthy and capable of independent life—carried for approximately 24 to 28 weeks. The wrongful death of that fetus is a recognized cause of action under the law.

Damages for Wrongful Death of a Child

The damages recoverable for the death of a child include medical, hospital and medication expenses, and the loss of consortium (love, companionship, services and support) that the child provided to the parents. The parents are also entitled to recover damages for the loss of financial support that the parents may have received from the child.

To recover lost financial support the parents will usually have to show a history of receiving support from the child before the child's death.

The parents may also recover damages for the loss of love and companionship of the child and for injury to or destruction of, the parent-child relationship. The actual amount recoverable will depend on the facts of an individual case but will typically depend on factors such as the age, health, and capacity of the child as well as the particular situation of the surviving parents.

Damages for the loss of love and companionship of the child and for injury to or destruction of the parent-child relationship may also encompass recovery for the parents' own grief, mental anguish, or suffering caused by the death of their child. These damages may be reflected in each parent's need for individual expenses caused by the child's death such as the expense of reasonable and necessary psychological treatment, counseling, and medication. Oftentimes it will be important to present expert psychiatric or psychological testimony to support the parent's claim for these damages.

Selecting an attorney in a case involving a child is very important as they should have experience settling or litigating these delicate types of cases. One challenging aspect of a case involving the wrongful death of a child is in proving the amount of damages the parents may be entitled to receive.

Chapter 5
Wrongful Death from an Auto Accident

If you have lost a loved one in a fatal auto accident there are actions you can take despite the unfortunate reality that nothing you do will bring back your loved one. But your family does have legal options including securing monetary compensation for items such as doctor bills, funeral costs, pain and suffering and a variety of other economic and non-economic damages.

When a person is killed in an automobile accident because of the negligence or fault of someone else, there can be a claim for wrongful death. In Ohio, it is required that the decedent's "personal representative" bring a wrongful death lawsuit. A personal representative can be either the executor or administrator of the decedent's estate.

This representative is the only person with authority to bring a claim, and this individual does so on behalf of the spouse, children or other next of kin (such as parents, siblings and grandparents).

Family members are often far too grief-stricken to negotiate the legal courses that are involved in a wrongful death claim. Still, if there is a surviving spouse or young children left behind, legal action against the party at fault might be essential to provide for their financial security in the future.

Chapter 6
Wrongful Death Resulting from the Failure of a Product

If someone you love has died in a manner related to a damaged or defective product on the market today, it is frustrating to make peace with reality. You are likely confused and angry. And while nothing can resolve such a situation completely, the law does provide for recourse against companies selling damaged or defective products. This may help you find closure and relief in the form of an action for wrongful death under the Ohio Product Liability Act. This Act applies to deaths occurring on or after April 7, 2005.

Under the Act, the representative of a deceased individual can seek compensatory damages from a manufacturer, retailer or other supplier of a product which is found to have caused a death.

It provides that a claimant may seek compensatory damages for economic loss resulting from the wrongful death of another, provided such damages arose from a defect in the:

(1) Manufacture or construction of the product;
(2) Design or formulation;
(3) Failure to warn or provide adequate instructions;
(4) A representation or warranty of the product.

Establishing each of the elements listed above and the damages applicable under this type of claim is typically based on the presentation of facts specific to a case.

An Ohio lawyer experienced with wrongful death cases and claims can advise you on your rights to bring lawsuits that can help ease the financial burden of economic losses you may have incurred because of a death related to a product.

Chapter 7
Wrongful Death from Explosions

Accidents resulting in explosions can cause extreme devastation. Whether they occur in the workplace, home, or a public area, explosions create a potential for loss of life.

Workplace explosions are among the most common. And particularly devastating are mining accidents where gases build and become trapped. In some cases, a spark from a piece of machinery can set off explosions that have been known to cause death or injury.

Construction sites and factories are also common scenes for explosion accidents. Compressed tanks filled with liquid propane, oxygen, acetylene and diesel fuel are frequently used by workers to weld or cut through metal. Employers are required by law to provide a safe work environment for their employees but often corners are cut to save money or equipment is not properly maintained.

City streets and commercial buildings can also be scenes of explosion accidents. Aging underground pipes or those tucked within walls may develop gas leaks.

We tend to consider our homes as a sanctuary from the dangers of the outside world, but these are unfortunately also prime locations for explosion accidents. Water heaters can explode from heat building up inside them. Defective appliances and propane tanks used for cooking and heating are among the many other sources of potential explosions.

When a person files a claim due to an explosion accident they need to establish three things: duty, breach, and cause. Duty occurs when the defendant owes a "duty" of safety. Breach occurs when that duty is not fulfilled. And cause means that the breach of duty directly led to the accident.

Chapter 8
Determining the Value of a Wrongful Death Case

Among the most important items in a wrongful death case is the issue of determining a reasonable estimation of what the case may be worth.

The decision to file a claim involves considering the following:

(1) An evaluation of how much one can expect to recover;

(2) How much it will cost in terms of time, money, and emotion to pursue the case through litigation and trial;

(3) An estimate of one's probability of success (i.e. determining how difficult it will be to convince a claims adjuster or a jury).

If someone is responsible for destroying your car, the car can be replaced. This is not the case when a human life is lost. There simply is no replacement for losing a child, parent, grandparent, husband or wife.

Keep in mind that the value of a wrongful death claim is not the same as placing a tangible value on the person who died. It is important to distinguish the difference between the value of a claim and the value of a person. The value of a person is priceless. The value of a claim, however, can be legally defined and determined.

Let's examine three different scenarios that demonstrate how the value of a wrongful death case varies depending on the circumstances and details of each as outlined below.

Scenario 1:

Suzie is walking with her friends to elementary school and crosses a street in the crosswalk. When she is in the middle of the crosswalk, a truck driver who is driving the truck of a nationally recognized delivery company runs a red light and hits Suzie. She dies a short time later while being transported via helicopter to the hospital. The driver had been working two consecutive shifts for the past five days to catch up on deliveries.

In this scenario, the truck driver is at fault and his employer is also going to be held responsible for the driver's actions. The employer is a large corporation and has nearly limitless resources to pay damages in this case. Juries are usually prejudiced against people who run red lights and against large corporations who place demands on their employees that create unsafe situations for the public. One might easily assume that the jury will probably want to punish the delivery company and the driver. This wrongful death case could be very substantial.

Scenario 2:

Suzie is walking with her friends to elementary school and crosses a street in the crosswalk. When she is in the middle of the crosswalk an elderly woman driving to a morning church service runs a red light and hits Suzie. Suzie dies later while being transported to the hospital. The elderly woman has very little money and depends on her monthly Social Security checks for income. Social Security benefits cannot be taken to satisfy a judgment. She has an auto insurance policy with minimum coverage.

In this scenario, the elderly woman is also at fault, but the case is entirely different than in the first Scenario. If this case goes to trial, a jury's verdict may be affected by their sympathy toward the elderly woman.

Scenario 3:

Suzie is playing basketball with her elementary school friends in the front driveway of her home. The basketball rolls into the middle of the street and Suzie runs between the middle of two cars parked on the street to get it. She darts out in front of a mother of three young children driving a minivan on her way home from the grocery store. The mother was traveling below the posted speed limit, but she did not see Suzie run into the street and hits her. Suzie dies a short time later while being transported to the hospital.

In this scenario, Suzie is probably at fault or at least shares a significant portion of the fault. The mother of three young children is a sympathetic defendant if the case was brought to trial. A jury may have more compassion and understanding toward the mother and determine she could not have seen Suzie to avoid the accident. Therefore, this case may have little or no value.

In each of these examples we have the same young girl who dies. Her parents suffer the same tragic loss regardless of the facts in each example. Yet the value of the wrongful death case in Scenario 1 is likely very high, in Scenario 2 the value is likely worth only the amount of the elderly woman's auto insurance policy and the value of the wrongful death case in Scenario 3 might very well have little or no value.

These scenarios are mere examples with limited details. In an actual wrongful death case there are numerous facts and issues that impact the value of a claim.

An Ohio wrongful death attorney will thoroughly evaluate how the facts and legal issues impact the value of a case and then discuss this evaluation with the client. In most cases, the attorney will need to conduct a thorough investigation and hire experts as well as take depositions before forming an accurate and reliable opinion regarding case value.

Determining Factors for the Value of a Claim

An examination of the primary factors that determine the value of a claim involve:

(1) The value of a case under the laws of Ohio.

This depends on the number of claimants involved as well as the damages that are recoverable.

The death of a single, childless 20-year-old man who is a high school dropout and unemployed may be worth little in monetary terms compared, say, to the wrongful death of a 50-year-old physician who is a husband and also a father of four children. Doctors typically earn a substantial amount of income and the claim may be significant.

(2) The jury's perception of you.

Whether or not a jury will have sympathy for a claimant is not as influential a factor as whether a jury will like you. What prejudices will the jury have for or against you? Do jurors know someone who has suffered a loss such as yours? The unwritten rule in personal injury law is that all things being equal, juries tend to give money to people they both like and respect. If the deceased's surviving family members come across as likeable, trustworthy, respectable, and genuinely sympathetic, then the jury is likely to award a higher verdict than if family members appear dishonest, unlikeable, or unsympathetic. If the jury perceives the survivors are using the lawsuit to try and "get rich," the returned verdict may be disappointing. But if the jury believes the survivors have suffered and endured much grief and loss as a result of their loved one's death, the verdict is apt to be a satisfactory one given the other facts and legal issues involved.

(3) The jury's perception of the deceased.

Whether the deceased was a "good person" or if you enjoyed a close relationship with the deceased are factors that weigh on a jury's perspective in awarding a claim. It is human nature to feel it is easier to give more money for the death of a nice person than it is for someone who is perceived as not being a good person societally.

(4) The amount of funds available to pay your claims.

In most situations when the defendant (the wrongdoer, the person, or company you're making a claim against) is either a person or a small company, the realistic maximum amount of money that can be collected is directly related to the amount of the available insurance held to cover your claims.

(5) The venue of your case.

A jury in a sparsely populated rural county tends to judge the value of a case differently than would a jury in a heavily populated urban area. Some trial courts move cases along quickly while others take many years to get a case to the trial stage.

(6) The judge and jury.

The judge has a considerable amount of discretion concerning what evidence will be let in or kept out, at trial. You may also draw a conservative jury as opposed to a more liberal one and each might value the case differently.

(7) The experience and skills of your lawyer.

Some lawyers have handled many different types of wrongful death cases, so they will likely be more versed in the law that covers these types of claims. The skill of your lawyer will have a great impact on the eventual value of a claim.

Chapter 9
Loss of Consortium
How it Factors into Wrongful Death Cases

Loss of consortium is the loss related to relationships and family-based issues. Consortium is comprised of three categories including loss of services, loss of support, and loss of marital relationship.

Loss of services refers to the spouse losing the help around the house that the plaintiff participated in before their injury. This includes things such as cleaning, laundry, dishes, lawn mowing, and other household chores.

Loss of support is the amount of money that the deceased would have contributed to the household. It is separate from the lost wages of the plaintiff which are part of the economic damages. To estimate this amount, the judge or jury would consider how much annual income the deceased person generated before the accident and then estimate a reasonable life expectancy had they not died.

Loss of marital relationship relates to the love and emotional support that the spouse loses. In other words, it is the support, affection, companionship and other non-economic-based losses that the spouse suffers from the death of his or her loved one.

Damages for the loss of the relationship with the deceased are purely subjective. The strength of the person's relationship right before death is extremely important. With surviving children, the age and the dependency on the deceased parent at the time of death are also very important factors. Younger children are usually more emotionally dependent on their parents so the damages for a younger child's loss of relationship will usually be much greater than if the child were older and more mature.

The perception of the value related to the loss of a relationship is the perceived closeness between the claimant and the deceased. How strong was their relationship? How long had they known each other? What did they do together? How often did they talk and see each other? Did they work together or play together? Was the deceased taking care of the claimant's needs as a caretaker or nurse? Was the deceased adept at listening to the claimant's troubles and providing him or her with sound advice, and making his or her life easier?

If the claimant is a spouse, what was the quality of the marriage? If the claimant is a child, what was the quality of the parent-child relationship? All these questions are considered when it comes to evaluating the amount of damages recoverable for the loss of the relationship with the deceased.

Chapter 10
Filing a Wrongful Death Claim with an Insurance Company

When a wrongful death takes place, the insurance claims process usually begins immediately. This means the personal representative and/or surviving family members must also take immediate action.

This should include, as necessary, preserving all the evidence from the accident, hiring experts to inspect any vehicles and/or the accident scene and obtaining witness statements. Many times, important evidence is lost if such actions are not taken immediately.

If there is a dispute as to the facts of an accident, you will need to make certain the at-fault party does not destroy any critical evidence or information. You can assume the insurance company is looking out for its interest. This fact makes it very important for you to look out for your own. What the insurance company wants and what would be best for the surviving family members are not often the same outcome

Although the police may investigate an accident, their investigative materials may not be available for a long period of time. In other instances, the police investigation may not be completely thorough or not address certain issues and questions that could be important or relevant in a wrongful death case. Evidence that would be vital for a civil case is not necessarily the same evidence that is crucial to forwarding a criminal case, which the police tend to focus on more during their work.

Every available piece of information should be gathered and kept so that it can be reviewed later either by an expert or an attorney. Experts know what evidence to collect, how to preserve it, and how to evaluate the importance or relevance of that evidence.

The Insurance Claims Process

The insurance adjuster assigned to your case is charged with trying to settle the claim expediently and at a low dollar figure before you have a true understanding of the claim and what it may be worth. What may seem like a large sum of money can be an inadequately low amount, relatively speaking.

Sometimes the adjuster will attempt to settle quickly to prevent you from hiring an attorney who could better represent your interests. The insurance company knows an adept attorney will likely have better leverage when negotiating a wrongful death case and can recover much more money than they are offering initially.

Your best interests and the interests of the insurance company are not the same. Insurance companies are looking for any reason they can to deny or minimize a claim. The insurance company cannot be trusted to protect the surviving family members' interests, no matter how compassionate and caring the insurer's representative may seem.

Filing a Wrongful Death Claim

If the death involves an auto accident, the first step is to contact your insurance agent and let him or her know that an accident has taken place. In most other accident cases you should contact the at-fault party or that party's insurance company, and you will want to obtain the claim number from them. If a claim has not been opened, you will want to give the carrier some basic information about what occurred. This may include the date and location of the accident as well as the names of the individuals involved.

You may instinctively want to delay talking to an insurance adjuster about the specifics of the claim until the initial shock has worn off regarding your tragic loss. It is difficult to believe, but there are insurance adjusters who will use a family member's shock and grief to their advantage. If you are distraught and overwhelmed by the loss of a loved one, you might say or do things that will impact the claim in the future. Statements you make about the deceased or what happened in the accident can be used against you at a later time.

Speaking with the Insurance Claims Adjuster

When pursuing a wrongful death claim you will likely be interviewed by a representative from your own insurance company, the deceased's carrier, the at-fault person's insurance company or by all three. You might think the adjuster is trying to help you especially if they are from your insurance company. But each insurance company adjuster owes his or her allegiance to the insurance company, not to you. Consider the following recommendations when talking to an insurance representative:

- Prepare for the meeting by speaking with an attorney. Take the time to fully understand the process and make the most of your attorney's expertise and experience.

- Before you get started with the interview, write down the name, address and phone number of the insurance adjuster and insurance company.

- Provide your full name, address and telephone number to the adjuster.

- If possible record the conversation. If you cannot record it, take good notes.

- Ask the adjuster if he or she is aware of any witnesses to the accident.

- Tell the truth. It is imperative that you are truthful always during the interview. Lying or exaggerating can be harmful to the claim.

- It is okay to answer, "I do not know" or "I don't understand."

- Be cordial and treat the adjuster with respect but be firm and assertive when necessary.

- Answer questions with "yes" or "no" that require it. Not every answer requires follow-up, so try and avoid rambling when answering questions.

Things You Should Not Do

- Do not agree to have the conversation recorded by the insurance adjuster unless your attorney is present for the interview, whether in person or also on the call by telephone.

- Insurance adjusters will try to engage you in an informal conversation to have you relax and get as many details about the accident as possible. Be aware of this tactic.

- Do not agree to anything. The interview should be about collecting information, NOT about your agreement to anything.

- **DO NOT SIGN ANYTHING.** No matter what the insurance adjuster faxes or mails to you, never sign any sort of document. Instead, give all documents to your attorney for review.

- Remember that during an interview with the adjuster you are not obligated to identify witnesses.

- Avoid talking in absolutes. In other words, do not give exact distances, times, etc. Always use qualifying words such as "approximately" when describing the details surrounding the accident.

- When you report the accident, give general information. You should always speak with your attorney before giving a formal recorded statement.

- Do not argue with or get angry at the adjuster. This will make it much more difficult to obtain a fair settlement of your case.

- Do not guess at the meaning of any question. If you do not understand what is being asked, request that the question be repeated or clarified. "I don't know" is usually an adequate answer if you don't understand the meaning of the question.

- Do not volunteer information. Make sure you fully answer the adjusters' question and then quit speaking. Although it is important to always tell the truth, it is also important not to give more information in your answer than necessary.

- Do not interrupt when the interviewer is asking the question even if you think you already know the answer.

- Do not allow the adjuster to assume facts that are not true when asking his question. Always correct or clarify any untrue facts.

- Do not give long, narrative answers. Short and concise answers are best.

How Does the Insurance Company Operate?

In its most simplistic form, the insurance company must take in more money than it pays out. An insurance company will focus on selling more policies and minimizing its liabilities. Any claim is a liability because the insurance company has to pay out money to settle the claim. The insurance adjuster's job is to settle claims for as little as possible while other people working for the company try to sell more policies.

If the adjuster can spot a defense or weakness in your claim, then his or her job is to make sure the defense or weakness is exploited fully so the insurance company can limit any payout. Sometimes an insurance adjuster can manufacture a defense or claim in the case. This is done by obtaining favorable statements from you and other witnesses.

To achieve your goal of recovering a fair and reasonable settlement you must provide the insurance adjuster with strong reasons that it should pay out more to settle the claim rather than less. This may be accomplished by providing the adjuster with certain information or documentation to support your claim. There are certain pieces of information that may be more persuasive than others. How relevant the information depends on the facts of the case and the status of the law that applies to the claim. Keep in mind that the more compelling the evidence submitted to support the claim, the higher the likelihood it will result in a more favorable settlement recovery.

How Claims are Evaluated

Statistically, more than 90 percent of all wrongful death claims are settled prior to trial – either during the claims process or during the litigation period before a trial. A fair and reasonable settlement may be successfully negotiated if your claim is properly documented, presented, and argued to the insurance adjuster. To do this, factors may include:

1. **The facts of the accident giving rise to the claim.** If the at-fault party's actions are shockingly bad, the claim may be valued higher than if the acts amounted only to a simple mistake.

2. **Identity of the parties.** If the death was caused by the actions of a sympathetic person (an elderly grandmother) then the claim may be lower than if

the death was caused by an unsympathetic party (a large corporation).

3. **The cause of death is important.** The claim may be worth more if the cause of death is uncontested. Similarly, if there are other explanations or prior medical conditions that could have contributed to the person's death, the value of the case may be lower.

4. **The number and status of the beneficiaries.** Usually, the value of a case is higher when the deceased was married with children. This is because each beneficiary has a right to claim compensation for the loss of the relationship.

5. **Pre-death suffering.** The value of the claim may be higher if the deceased experienced conscious pain and suffering before death. Typically, the longer the period of time experienced the higher the value of the claim.

6. **Liability defenses.** If the at-fault person can successfully prove that he or she was not at fault or that someone else was at fault, then the value of the claim might be lowered significantly.

7. **Information about the deceased.** If there exists damaging or embarrassing information about the

deceased (the deceased was not considered a good person, had criminal convictions, etc.), then the value of the claim may be less.

8. **The existence, or lack of, insurance coverage.** There must be enough coverage to pay for all of the damages. If the at-fault driver was uninsured, you may not recover anything (assuming you have no additional coverage such as uninsured motorists or UM). If the other driver only had minimal coverage, then this may be all that you receive (unless additional coverage exists).

9. **The experience and reputation of your lawyer.** If you have an experienced lawyer who regularly handles wrongful death claims representing you, this may increase the value of your claim in the eyes of the insurance company.

There is no magic formula for placing a value on the loss of a human life. Much of the loss or the amounts of damages that are legally recoverable are purely subjective in nature. The value of a claim is heavily influenced by the quality of the relationship between the deceased and the surviving spouse and/or children. Ultimately, the value of any given case is what a jury says it is. No two cases are alike and each one must be judged on its own merits given the facts.

The Settlement Package

When it comes to representing surviving family members in a wrongful death case, Slater & Zurz LLP goes to extraordinary lengths to compile and present an effective settlement demand package to the insurance company. We obtain all documents and materials that may relate to the claim and then organize and present them in the most influential and persuasive way possible to secure the highest recovery.

The settlement demand package may include many different types of documents, records and other items, including:

- A complete discussion and analysis of the facts of the accident and the wrongful death laws that may apply;

- Incident reports or police reports;

- Copies of pleadings that are ready to be filed in court if the settlement does not occur (a complaint, or deposition notice, etc.);

- Photos of the scene of the accident or of the injuries;

- Medical records and reports;

- Expert report findings;

- Re-enactments and/or computer simulations;

- Testimony from witnesses and/or experts;

- Audio and/or video recordings;

- Presentations showcasing the facts of a case;

- Witness statements.

By providing a comprehensive settlement package, you are helping the insurance adjuster build his or her file so that the company can justify paying out a large settlement.

Providing this sort of package gives the insurance company many reasons for settling the claim immediately rather than going to court.

Settlement vs. Trial

Your primary goal during the claims process is to build your case by collecting and evaluating all the evidence that can help you secure a fair and reasonable settlement. There are many benefits and advantages to settling a case, including:

- **Avoiding the risk of trial.** Litigation is risky because juries are unpredictable. It doesn't matter how strong you think the case may be, a jury can always come up with arguments or reasons to justify a lower verdict or to side with the insurance company. Going to trial is always going to be a gamble to a certain extent.

- **Avoiding the expense of litigation and trial.** Wrongful death cases are expensive to pursue. Attorney ethics rules require that the expense of litigation must be borne by the client although the attorney may advance these costs. Most of the expenses can come from hiring experts, paying for depositions, and creating trial exhibits.

- **Achieving final resolution of the claim and gaining peace of mind.** There is certainly an emotional toll on family members who must participate in the litigation of a case. These cases also impose time requirements on family members. They may have to take time off work to attend a deposition and/or attend trial dates.

- **Avoiding further emotional pain.** It can be difficult for family members to "re-live" the circumstances surrounding the death of their loved one. The litigation experience can delay closure and may bring up painful feelings of grief and sorrow, repeatedly. The grieving process may be stalled in ways until the case has officially concluded.

The disadvantage to agreeing to a settlement could be that you will never know what the jury would have done. It comes down to whether you want to take a chance at going to trial. The pros and cons of litigation and trial must be carefully weighed so that you can make the best decision for your family. Each case is different, of course, and involves varying legal questions that must be answered.

Chapter 11
How Wrongful Death Cases are Litigated

The laws and procedures governing wrongful death claims are complex. This also holds true for the litigation process in a case as the rules governing litigation are often entirely dependent on the laws and procedures in the local jurisdiction. That is why it is extremely important that family members consult with an Ohio attorney who has experience litigating wrongful death cases if they live in the state.

Filing a Lawsuit

To file a wrongful death lawsuit, many documents must be provided to the court. The complaint sets forth the facts that support the claim along with a description or statement of the legal theories that are being alleged against the wrongdoer. The complaint will typically identify the parties, the facts or circumstances surrounding the person's death and the specific laws which support or authorize the cause of action being brought to the court.

The person who files a wrongful death lawsuit is called the "plaintiff" while the person or party being sued is called the "defendant."

The lawsuit is usually divided into different stages: (1) information gathering or discovery phase, (2) pre-trial preparation stage, (3) pre-trial settlement or alternative dispute resolution stage, and (4) trial.

The length of each of these stages or phases will depend on the complexity of the case as well as the laws and rules of the local jurisdiction where the case is being prosecuted.

In Ohio, a wrongful death lawsuit must usually be filed in the court of the county where either the death occurred or where one of the defendants resides. Each county has its own court. Each court may also have its own local rules about filing deadlines and setting trial dates.

The court will also have guidelines in place for motion practice. There are numerous motions that may need to be filed in a case concerning issues of law that must be decided by the judge. These issues may involve discovery matters, legal questions, and evidence questions.

Statute of Limitations

A wrongful death lawsuit must be filed in court within a certain period of time. This period is often called the statute of limitations. Depending on the jurisdiction, the statute of limitations may begin to run on the date of death, upon discovery of the person's cause of death or upon discovery of a defendant's negligent conduct.

The length of the statute of limitations period will vary depending on the laws of the jurisdiction that govern the wrongful death claim.

It is a dangerous practice to wait until the statute of limitations period is about to expire before filing a wrongful death lawsuit. If the lawsuit is filed right before the deadline, or if the defendant cannot be found or the wrong defendant is served, the case could be dismissed, and the plaintiff receives no compensation of any kind.

Another reason not to wait until the statute of limitations is about to expire is that important evidence in the case may be lost or destroyed. Witness memories can fade over time or important witnesses may move and be difficult to locate. The more time that elapses after a death, the greater the likelihood important evidence may be lost or destroyed. In short, waiting too long to investigate or prosecute the claim in court may cause irreparable damage to the case.

Authority to File a Lawsuit

Ohio law requires a personal representative be appointed on behalf of the deceased's estate. This person acts on behalf of the deceased and is given authority by the court to file suit for the purpose of recovering damages in a lawsuit. A wrongful death lawsuit cannot be prosecuted until a personal representative is appointed by the court.

Oftentimes the personal representative is a surviving family member or a good friend of the deceased. Sometimes a professional such as another lawyer can be appointed as the personal representative.

In one claim an action is brought to recover damages on behalf of the estate (funeral and healthcare expenses, the deceased's lost future earnings, etc.). In another claim, a lawsuit can be brought to recover damages for each surviving beneficiary. A surviving spouse may recover separate damages for the destruction of the marital relationship. Each surviving child may recover separate damages for the loss of the parent-child relationship. The damages claimed by each beneficiary are considered distinct and separate from the damages claimed by the estate.

The personal representative who brings the case will have a fiduciary obligation to the other interested parties in the action (other beneficiaries). This means that the personal representative has a legal duty to protect the interests of the estate and all beneficiaries who may have a right to recover damages in the case. The failure to fulfill this duty may subject the personal representative to legal liability.

The Discovery Process

After the lawsuit is filed and the defendant is served notice, both sides participate in a process of exchanging information about the case. This process is known as discovery. There are many different forms of discovery or different ways to request or obtain information from the other side in a case. The rules governing the discovery process are quite broad and allow each side to investigate what evidence and witnesses may be introduced at trial. Even if the requested information does not appear directly relevant to the case it may still be a proper request if it leads to the discovery of relevant information.

One form of discovery may involve sending or answering written questions called interrogatories. There may also be written requests for production of documents and other materials that are deemed relevant to the claims being made in the suit. There may be limits to the number of written questions or requests that can be exchanged depending on the local court rules. When the interrogatories and requests for production are answered and completed, the personal representative or beneficiary must also execute a document stating that the answers and responses are true and accurate.

Another form of discovery may include a deposition. A deposition is a face-to-face meeting where the attorneys can ask witnesses questions under oath while a court reporter transcribes the session. Any witness who may offer testimony at trial can be deposed, including the personal representative, a beneficiary (or surviving family member), the deceased's doctor, the medical examiner or coroner, other family members, eyewitnesses, and experts otherwise involved in the case.

The deposition is a very important legal proceeding that should almost always involve preparation by the attorney and the person who is going to be deposed. The person's performance at the deposition can have a huge influence on the success or value of the case.

In addition to interrogatories, requests for production, and depositions, each side's lawyer may also be permitted to issue a subpoena. This is a request to produce documents or items in addition to requesting that the person appear at a deposition or trial.

The discovery phase can also include a request by the other side that the plaintiff or a beneficiary submits to a medical examination and/or a psychological evaluation. Ohio's discovery rules permit one party to request such for the purpose of learning more about the person's health and to evaluate their claim for damages.

The legal and factual grounds necessary to support a request to conduct a medical examination or psychological evaluation on a surviving family member will depend on the facts of the case and the issues involved. In most cases, the judge will have considerable discretion to grant or deny the request for a medical or psychological evaluation on a case-by-case basis.

Utilizing Expert Witnesses

After a case has been filed in court it will often require the assistance of expert testimony to help the attorney prove one or more elements of the action.

Since wrongful death cases can involve many different issues that can be complex and difficult to prove, an experienced attorney will want to engage the assistance of one or more experts early in the case. The success of a case may hinge on the credibility or knowledge of the experts involved. Therefore, it is extremely important that the attorney have substantial experience in handling wrongful death cases as well as having the knowledge of the different types of experts that may be necessary to achieve a successful outcome.

The term "economic damages" refers to those tangible damages that are considered easier to calculate such as lost wages, medical expenses, future income loss, or lost net accumulations to the deceased's estate. Examples of economic damage experts include economists, medical experts, accountants, vocational experts, and financial care and life planners.

One of the most common types of damages requested in a wrongful death case are claims for the deceased's future lost earnings or the future net lost accumulations to the person's estate. A vocational expert may be necessary to help establish the deceased's lost income and future occupational advancement opportunities. An economist or accountant may be necessary to calculate the present value of the future lost earnings based on the deceased's occupation at the time of death, anticipated future promotions, and the person's savings and consumption rate.

When utilizing experts to calculate economic damages, it is important to involve the expert early in the case and furnish them with all of the necessary documentation required to form an opinion.

The second category of damages consists of "non-economic damages" and refers to those subjective, or intangible types of loss that are often more difficult to quantify. They include pain, suffering, grief and the loss of the deceased's love, society, companionship and affection. It is wise to retain one or more experts to address or discuss these types of damages to a jury.

Take a case involving the death of a child. The parents will likely suffer a substantial amount of psychological distress and suffering. It may be beneficial to use a psychological expert such as a psychiatrist, psychologist, or mental health therapist to discuss the parents' loss of their child. There may be long-term emotional issues that surviving parents and children face as a result of losing a loved one prematurely. Using an expert to discuss, explain, and highlight these losses may be helpful in explaining the parents' loss to the jury.

Another category concerns the deceased's pre-death pain and suffering, as the law permits the estate to recover damages for such. If there is a dispute over whether the deceased did experience pain or fear before death, then a medical or psychological expert will be highly useful in establishing this fact.

The selection of an expert is a critically important factor that can have a huge influence on the success of any wrongful death case. Sometimes, the academic and professional credentials of the expert are extremely important. Other times the ability of the expert to teach and explain the field of expertise to a jury or layperson may be valued more highly than the expert's academic credentials or success. Choosing which expert will work best is a judgment call best made by the attorney and should be based on the specific needs of the case.

Attorneys must also take into consideration the expense of hiring and using experts. There must be a real need for the expert to engage one for a case. And above all else, the attorney must choose experts carefully and use them in their capacity to highlight or explain certain issues in the case.

There may only be a few qualified experts in a field of study, so an experienced attorney may wish to retain one or more of these experts immediately before the defense attorney can do so.

The unique facts and circumstances of the case will dictate which type of expert to use and how many experts will be necessary in a given case. Because experts are a critical component in a successful case, it is usually beneficial to retain an experienced attorney early on so there is sufficient time to locate, hire, and brief each expert who may be necessary to support the merits of the claim.

Depending on the jurisdiction and the complexity of a case, the discovery phase in litigation may take many months or sometimes even years to reach completion. When discovery is finally completed, and each side generally knows what evidence will be offered at trial, the parties may then begin to conduct settlement discussions. Sometimes the laws of the particular jurisdiction or venue will require the parties to engage in meaningful efforts to settle the case other than negotiating between themselves. These efforts are sometimes referred to as alternative dispute resolution. One example of this is mediation.

In mediation, the parties agree to hire an impartial person (called the mediator) to help them settle the case. Often the mediator is a retired judge or an experienced attorney who has advanced training and education.

The process of mediation is usually voluntary and non-binding (unless a settlement is reached). This means that a mediator cannot force a party to settle and either party is permitted to reject offers from the other side. The expectation here is that the parties will participate in mediation in good faith and with the goal of trying to settle the case instead of going to trial.

A mediation session is a confidential proceeding so that anything said during the session cannot be used at trial. Mediation can be successfully used to resolve a case involving wrongful death claims. These sessions can be held over the course of one day or several days depending on the size and complexity of the case.

Evaluating settlement offers at mediation depends on many factors. The experience of the attorney is often important because a settlement offer will always be judged in relation to how a jury may decide the case. You will want an attorney who has successfully litigated wrongful death cases in the past. Both sides will attempt to predict how a jury might rule and then factor this into their evaluation of the case.

Preparing for Trial

If the case is not settled after discovery and mediation, then the case may proceed to trial.

Going to trial in a wrongful death case usually requires a tremendous amount of resources, time and preparation. The attorney invests a substantial amount of money and time in the case to conduct depositions, hire and prepare experts, create trial exhibits, and draft and prepare the necessary documents that must be filed in court.

The insurance companies and their attorneys know how expensive and time-consuming a case is to pursue. They may use this fact to their advantage by intentionally delaying resolution of the case over a long period of time.

The trial of a wrongful death case is usually more complex than other types of accident cases. There are typically more experts and other witnesses involved which means a trial can easily take weeks or months to conclude.

Add to this the fact that a trial can be much more physically and emotionally exhausting for all parties involved. A person's life has been lost due to someone else's negligence. As a result, people's emotions usually run very high.

Sometimes the insurance company will go to extensive efforts to fight the case or attempt to minimize the damages being claimed. The case can also involve multiple claims with high potential values, causing the insurance company to believe it is in its best interests to defend the case vigorously when so much money is at stake.

A defendant's insurance carrier may make a settlement offer that is considered on the low-end of a reasonable settlement range on the theory that the attorney will not want to incur the substantial expense and time of going to trial to increase that initial offer. Therefore, it is preferable that the case is handled by an experienced and competent attorney who not only has the expertise to pursue the claim, but also the financial resources to take the case all the way through a trial if necessary.

Still, it is true that most people do want to avoid going through with a trial. They are stressful and can cause additional anxiety for everyone involved. A trial is usually the last resort to resolve the claim. The insurance company will not want a serious or significant case to go to trial particularly when there is not a serious dispute about the defendant's negligence and the cause of death.

Some insurance companies have a reputation for utilizing specific tactics to prolong the litigation process to wear down the attorney and the family so that they will accept a smaller settlement.

It is only by threatening to advance the case and thoroughly preparing for trial that an attorney can secure a reasonable and fair settlement offer for the estate and each surviving beneficiary.

You don't want to hire a lawyer for a case only to find out a few weeks or months before trial that the lawyer has limited experience handling wrongful death cases or has never tried a significant case in court.

Chapter 12
Contingency Fee Agreements with Attorneys

Many people are reluctant to speak with or hire an attorney because of their perceived cost of doing so. They simply cannot afford to write checks for thousands of dollars every month during the process waiting for a settlement or a verdict in their case.

Fortunately, there is an arrangement that exists in which you can utilize the experience and knowledge of a professional attorney without needing to pay monthly legal fees while your wrongful death claim is being pursued.

Our law firm, like many others, represents clients on what is known as a contingency-fee basis. With a contingency fee agreement, a lawyer will defer his or her fees until the case is successfully resolved and finalized. The fee is based on a percentage of the settlement or verdict obtained in the case. If no settlement is received or no amount is awarded in a verdict, there will be no fees paid to the attorney.

Contingency fees also allow people to hire the best legal representation possible without the risk of losing thousands and thousands of dollars.

As mentioned throughout this book, the insurance company employs a team of professionals looking out for its best interest to try and deny or minimize claims. A contingency fee arrangement allows you to employ your own experienced legal professionals that will fight for you and protect your interests.

There is no reason for you not to at least speak with an experienced lawyer. You are under no obligation to hire the attorney and a simple conversation may give you a much better understanding of how best to proceed with your claim.

A fear of the unknown prevents a lot of people from moving forward and getting themselves out of troublesome situations. We sincerely hope this book has given you a basic understanding of your rights under Ohio law and a sense of real understanding and sound legal advice on how to proceed.

If you would like to talk to us about a wrongful death case in the state of Ohio, we welcome your call. We can be reached via telephone at 1-800-297-9191, via email at slaterzurz@slaterzurz.com or on our website at slaterzurz.com.

The Authors

The Ohio law firm of Slater & Zurz LLP is a team of legal professionals dedicated to helping victims of all types of accidents and their families throughout Ohio. Our law firm has been entrusted to handle more than 30,000 personal injury cases since its founding and has helped clients receive more than $150 million in settlements and verdicts.

Attorney Jim Slater is the managing partner of Slater & Zurz LLP and has been actively practicing law for more than 40 years. When Mr. Slater is asked what the law firm of Slater & Zurz LLP does, he replies simply by saying:

We Make Others Do What They Do Not Want to Do.

We make the decision-makers at insurance companies pay fair and proper compensation to victims of accidents.

We make wayward partners pay those they treated unfairly.

We make individuals and businesses pay their customers and employees the money they owe them.

We provide comfort to families by financially punishing owners of nursing homes that harm their loved ones.

We convince juries to award our clients the money they deserve.

In all cases, we work tirelessly to be sure our clients get what they are entitled to receive.

Prior to asking for our help, our clients were either denied proper compensation or were uncertain whether they could receive the compensation they deserved.

We have made companies pay millions when they negligently manufactured products that caused serious injuries.

We have made insurance companies pay hundreds of thousands of dollars when the dogs of homeowners they insured attacked innocent children and caused serious injury.

We have made a hospital pay millions when one of their doctors caused a child's death.

We made a large company pay millions to its employees when they failed to pay the commission income they had earned.

At Slater & Zurz LLP, all cases do not involve millions or hundreds of thousands of dollars. Many of our cases involve smaller amounts of money. But there is a common theme. We make companies and people who have or would treat our clients unfairly do what they do not want to do.

This is what we do at Slater & Zurz LLP. This is what we have done for our more than 30,000 clients in 40 plus years of service. I am personally proud of the difference we make every day on behalf of our clients. It has been our goal, from the beginning, to make people proud that we are their attorney and pleased with the results we obtain for them. This is why we do what we do.

- **James W. Slater**

Free Consultations Are Always Offered at
Slater & Zurz LLP
Attorneys at Law
Serving Clients Throughout Ohio
From These Office Locations:
Akron • Canton • Cleveland • Columbus

Please call toll free
1-800-297-9191
or visit slaterzurz.com

More Free Books Available from Slater & Zurz LLP

We have written books on many different legal topics including the following:

When A Dog Bites Fight Back

Stop Nursing Home Abuse in Ohio

Motorcycle Crashes in Ohio

Trucking Accidents in Ohio

Legal Malpractice in Ohio

To request a free copy of any of our books, please call 1-800-297-9191 or send us a message from our website at slaterzurz.com.

www.ingramcontent.com/pod-product-compliance
Lightning Source LLC
Chambersburg PA
CBHW061516180526
45171CB00001B/200